# Fishing

GET OUTDOORS

WITHDRAWN

Nick
Ross

**PowerKiDS**
press

New York

Published in 2010 by The Rosen Publishing Group Inc.
29 East 21st Street, New York, NY 10010

First Edition

Library of Congress Cataloging-in-Publication Data

Ross, Nick, 1965-
    Fishing / Nick Ross.
        p. cm. — (Get outdoors)
    Includes index.
    ISBN 978-1-4358-3042-4 (library binding)
    ISBN 978-1-4358-3050-9 (paperback)
    ISBN 978-1-4358-3058-5 (6-pack)
    1.  Fishing—Juvenile literature.  I. Title.
    SH445.R675 2010
    799.1—dc22

                          2008051960


Manufactured in China

CPSIA Compliance Information: Batch #WA010150PK:
For Further Information contact Rosen Publishing, New York at 1-800-237-9932

Acknowledgements
The author and publisher would like to thank the following people
for participating in our photoshoot: Brian Syde (Banbury & District
Angling Club), Mike Stanley, Rozie Stanley, and Ben Rhodes.

All photography by Tudor Photography except
5 Bridgeman Art Library/Getty Images; 10, 11, 25 top, 25 left
i-StockPhoto;  24, 29 top Luka Lukman; 28 Peter and Barry Ayers;
29 bottom Georgette Douwma/Getty Images.

Note to parents
and teachers:

Disclaimer:
In the preparation of this
book, care has been
exercised with regard
to advice, activities and
techniques. However, when
the reader is learning
or engaged in a sport
or utilizing a piece of
equipment, the reader
should get advice from
an expert and follow the
manufacturer's instructions.
The publisher cannot be,
and is not liable for, any
loss or injury the reader
may sustain.

# Contents

# The world of fishing

Fishing is a popular sport all around the world, with millions of people taking part. In the United States alone, around fifty million people, young and old, participate. Whether you are on your own, or with friends or family, fishing is a great way to relax and spend time outdoors having fun. There are many branches of the sport to choose from; with challenges for all—from the most physical and active people, to those who like to sit quietly and enjoy the mental test of catching a fish.

## Choosing a branch

Each branch of fishing involves different techniques and slightly different equipment. Fishing for trout or salmon is called fly fishing, or game fishing, and sea fishing takes place from the seashore or off a boat or pier. The most popular branch of fishing is coarse fishing, which is fishing for freshwater fish, but not salmon and trout. Although this book looks at all three types, it focuses on coarse fishing.

## Early beginnings

Apart from being one of the most popular sports in the world, fishing is also one of the oldest sports on record. Thousands of years ago, prehistoric people caught fish for food. They used hooks made from animal bone. Later, in the 1400s, rods were made from ash, hazel, and willow wood, and lines were braided from horse hair.

*Around the world, fishing is enjoyed by men, women, boys, and girls.*

Fishing equipment improved greatly after the Industrial Revolution in the eighteenth century, and since then, rods and tackle have continued to develop to accommodate every kind of fishing imaginable.

## Match Fishing

To catch fish, you will need to concentrate, develop patience, and think hard about what you are doing. Successful match fishermen plan well and are organized and skilled—they are able to change tactics to suit the water, type of fish, and weather conditions. They learn to think like fish!

*Fishing for food dates back thousands of years. This wall painting is from the Tomb Chapel of Menna in the Valley of Nobels in Thebes, in Ancient Egypt.*

# How to get started

There are many places to go fishing, from ponds and lakes specially made for fishing, to canals and rivers, which have their own challenges. If you are over 12 years old, you may need to buy a fishing license. Some fishing waters are owned privately or by an angling club, with many offering junior day tickets or season tickets. Sometimes clubs prefer young people to be accompanied by an adult, so it is important to find out all the information you can before you set off.

## Choosing the right water

Some lakes have prepared fishing areas called "swims." Look for a swim that gives you some cover with "fishy" places such as lily beds, reeds, overhanging willow trees, and deeper water. Rivers offer a different challenge, because they can be unpredictable and varied, depending on where you fish. Your local river may be fast flowing, ideal for fish such as grayling, chub, dace, and barbel, or deep and slow, which is perfect for roach, rudd, and bream. Canals are often narrow, shallow, and slow moving, and hold a wide variety of fish. If you live near a river or a canal, find out more about it at your local tackle shop or by talking to an angler on the bank before you start fishing.

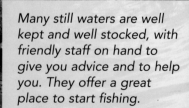

*Many still waters are well kept and well stocked, with friendly staff on hand to give you advice and to help you. They offer a great place to start fishing.*

## Environment Savvy

1. Take all your trash home or put it in a trash can. This includes old fishing line, weights, broken rigs, food wrappers, and soda cans.

2. Discarded fishing tackle is dangerous to wildlife—so carefully dispose it!

3. Make sure you fish in prepared swims to reduce damage to vegetation along the banks, and to avoid losing tackle.

4. Use barbless hooks (hooks without a second, backward pointing part) whenever possible.

5. Watch out for wildlife. Retrieve your line if birds are swimming nearby.

6. Do not leave your rod unattended.

7. Do not leave baited hooks on the river bank since they may be picked up by animals or birds.

## Taking care of the environment

Fishing is a natural sport, and the best places to fish are often full of a wide variety of wild animals and plant life. A wildlife guidebook and a pair of binoculars will help you to identify some of the creatures with whom you share the waterside. Anglers need to learn to fish quietly and respect the natural environment. Fish will quickly become nervous and move away if you make a lot of noise, so, like a hunter, always move slowly and carefully, disturbing as little as possible.

## The weather

Since fishing is a year-round outdoor pursuit, weather plays a big part, so always be prepared. Try to find out about the expected weather before you go fishing and always wear the right clothing. Wading boots or strong shoes with good grip are essential. Take a waterproof coat with you, just in case the weather turns bad. In the winter, wear a layered clothing system to keep you warm and dry. In really hot spells, save your fishing for the early morning and evening when the fish will feed. Use an umbrella for shade and a good sunscreen to avoid sunburn. Do not fish during thunderstorms, because fishing rods make very good lightning conductors! Instead, wait for the storm to pass and then get ready for some excellent fishing.

*Put all your trash in a trash can before you leave the swim. If there isn't one nearby, be sure to take your litter home with you.*

# Fishing equipment

At first glance, the range of equipment, or tackle, that you can buy may seem overwhelming. But fishing is a simple sport—the basic tackle that you will need is fairly cheap, and the skills that will help to get you started are easy to learn.

*Rods*—today's rods are made from a lightweight material such as carbon fiber, with handles made from cork or another waterproof material. Poles come in different lengths, and can be up to 26 feet (8 meters). The pole sections fit inside each other and are taken apart to allow the fish to be landed.

## Choosing a Rod

When choosing your rod, start with a general, all-purpose rod that is light, comfortable to hold, and that you can use in as many situations as possible. A float rod that is 9–11.5 feet (3–3.5 meters) long is ideal. Take care of your rod, and always clean it and put it away dry after use, to make it last as long as possible.

*Reels*—start by using a basic, fixed spool reel. The spool holds the line, while the bale arm traps the line for winding in and releasing for casting. The drag allows a strong fish to take line when it is hooked and stops the line from breaking. Set the drag so that the line is not too easy to pull off the spool, but so that it will not break when a strong fish tries to run.

*Line*—fishing line comes in a variety of strengths or "breaking strains." A good starting line for general fishing is about 2.8 pounds (1.3 kilograms). To load the reel, attach the line from the spool to the reel with a half blood knot (see page 11) and have someone hold the spool tightly while you reel it onto the spool carefully, making sure there is some tension so that it goes on neatly. Fill the reel to the lip of the spool.

keep net

**Disgorger**—use this to unhook a fish quickly and safely.

**Nets**—a keep net allows you to retain your fish for the day so that you can see what you have caught. If you are fishing in a competition, it also allows you to have your catch weighed. A landing net is essential and will allow you to land a good fish safely and easily once it is played out.

landing net

**Hooks**—these come in different sizes, from 1 (large) to 22 (small), for different baits, fish, and types of presentation. A good general hook is a size 14–16, but you should aim to have a variety of hooks in your tackle box.

**Bait box**—this is used to store bait.

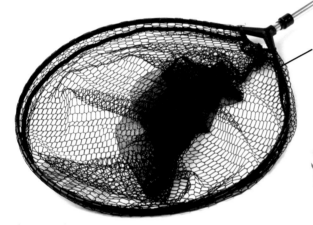

**Floats**—a few floats of different weights and sizes will get you started. A float allows you to present the bait to the fish at different levels in the water. Floats are also used to indicate a bite, which is why they are usually bright and highly visible. Floats are held down using weights called split shots, which are made of nontoxic metal. The amount of weight needed to cock the float will be printed on the side of the float. The largest (AAA) are called swan shot, and the smallest (no. 10) are called dust shot.

**Catapult**—use this with care to get loose feed out to your fishing spot with accuracy and distance.

**Ledger weights**—ledger weights take the bait to the bottom of the water and hold it there. You will need ledger weights if you fish in deep water and/or on windy days. Weights include arlsey bombs, coffin leads, and drilled bullets.

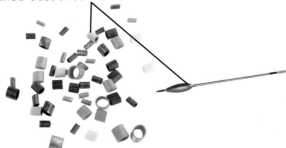

coffin leads

arlsey bombs

drilled bullets

# Types of fish

There are many different types of fish that can be caught using simple tackle. In addition to those illustrated here, there are many more that are worth reading about. These include the beautiful grayling, the little gudgeon, the powerful barbel, and a real monster... the massive catfish.

## Tench

**Specimen:** 2.9 lbs. (1.3 kg)

**Record:** 14 lbs. (6.5 kg)

**Location:** Still waters, canals and rivers

**Tactics:** Bottom feeders, ledgering or a float with the bait right on the bottom

**Line:** 4–5.5 lbs. (2–2.5 kg)

**Hook size:** 6–10

**Bait:** Worms, bread paste, corn, lunchmeat, or maggots

## Roach

**Specimen:** 2.2 lbs. (1 kg)

**Record:** 4 lbs. (1.9 kg)

**Location:** Rivers, canals, ponds, and lakes

**Tactics:** Float fishing or ledgering

**Line:** 2.2–3 lbs. (1–1.5 kg)

**Hook size:** 14–20

**Bait:** Bread flake or paste, single maggot, or cloudy mix groundbait

## Bream

**Specimen:** 4 lbs. (1.8 kg)

**Record:** 18 lbs. (8.3 kg)

**Location:** Slow rivers, canals, and lakes

**Tactics:** Bottom feeders or ledgering

**Line:** 2.9–4 lbs. (1.3–1.9 kg)

**Hook size:** 8–12

**Bait:** Worms, maggots, bread paste, or flake

## Carp

**Specimen:** 4.4 lbs. (2 kg)

**Record:** 66 lbs. (30 kg)

**Location:** Still waters, canals, and rivers

**Tactics:** Floats, poles, ledgering, freelining, or surface fishing

**Line:** 4.5 lbs. (2 kg), or 9 lbs. (4 kg) and a powerful rod for bigger fish)

**Hook size:** 4–12

**Bait:** Worms, sweetened bread paste, corn, lunchmeat, bread crust, dog biscuits, or boilies

## Pike

**Specimen:** 11 lbs. (5 kg)

**Record:** 46 lbs. (21 kg)

**Location:** Rivers, weirs, reed beds, lakes, canals, and reservoirs

**Tactics:** Ledgering, float fishing, or spinning. Use a wire trace to stop the pike from biting through the line.

**Line:** 11 lbs. (5 kg)

**Hook size:** Treble hook in 6–12

**Bait:** Small dead fish, such as sprats, pilchards, mackerel, or roach

## Perch

**Specimen:** 2.2 lbs. (1 kg)

**Record:** 5.5 lbs. (2.5 kg)

**Location:** Lakes ponds, canals, and slower, deeper, rivers

**Tactics:** Float fishing, ledgering, or spinning

**Line:** 3 lbs. (1.5 kg)

**Hook size:** 8–14

**Bait:** Worms, maggots, or spinners with a wire trace only

## Unhooking Perch

Perch have sharp spines on their dorsal fin (the main fin on the spine). To unhook the fish, sweep the fin down from the head, pressing the spines down flat toward the tail. Hold the fish firmly on the side as you take out the hook.

# Bait

Different types of fish prefer different baits. Depending on what you are hoping to catch, you will need to prepare a range of bait, from maggots and worms, to corn and bread.

## Maggots

Most fish will bite if you use maggots as bait. Maggots are the small, wriggly grubs of bluebottle flies. If you look closely enough, you will see that a maggot has a blunt end and a sharp end. To secure your bait, place the hook through the skin gently at the blunt end.

## Bread

Bread is very good bait for roach, rudd, carp, tench, and bream. It can be used in flakes, crusts, or pastes to secure your catch. Try cutting up the crust in cubes as big as your thumb and using them on the surface of the water for carp. Bread flake is made by taking a pinch of bread from the middle of a white loaf, and squeezing it onto the hook to leave it fluffy and attractive to the fish. Try making bread paste by taking a big slice of white bread without the crusts, wrapping it in a cloth, and wetting it with water from your swim. Squeeze it until it forms a firm paste, then mold it onto the hook. You could add honey or other flavors to the bread to tempt fish.

## Worms

Fish love worms! Lobworms are one of the biggest garden varieties and are great bait for carp, tench, bream, eels, perch, and barbel. Red worms and brandlings are often found in good compost heaps, and are smaller and attractive to many fish.

## Corn

Buy large-grain corn and put one or more grains on the hook. Add some loose feed and the sweet smell will attract carp, tench, roach, and bream.

## Lunchmeat

Meat is a great bait for big fish such as carp, tench, barbel, and bream. Cut the meat into cubes and thread the hook through it carefully. Fish the bait with a ledger rig (see page 23) and add a few pieces as loose feed to attract big fish.

## Cheese

If you are after chub, try cheese. A small piece of hard cheese, such as cheddar, molded onto the hook will work wonders.

## Fish

If you want to catch pike, a small fish, such as mackerel, is the bait to use. Pike are sometimes called freshwater sharks because of their size, strength, and sharp teeth.

## Boilies, dog biscuits, pepperoni

Flavored baits, including pastes, pellets, and boilies, are very popular and many varieties can be bought from a tackle shop.

## Groundbait

Groundbait is essential because it attracts fish into your swim and keeps them there. Buy bags of ready-made groundbait at your tackle shop—the cheapest is breadcrumbs. Mix the groundbait with water to form a ball that can be loose to make a cloudy mix or heavy to make a sinking mix that will get to the bottom of a river with a current. You can add flavors such as vanilla or strawberry to make your own secret recipe.

# Using the equipment

Once you have the basic equipment, you can get ready to fish! Set up your tackle away from the water's edge. Take your time and think about the weather conditions, the water, and the type of fish you hope to catch. When you're ready, move slowly into position.

## Setting up

**1**

Put the rod sections together and fix the reel to the rod handle or butt.

**2**

Make sure all the rod eyes are in a straight line.

**3**

Open the bale arm on the reel so that the line pulls off the reel.

**4**

Thread the line through ALL of the rod eyes.

**5**

Attach the end rig for ledgering or float fishing, depending on what fish you want to catch.

**6**

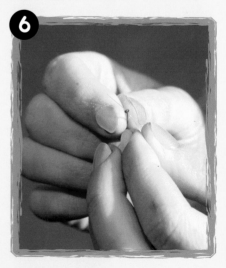

Tie on the hook.

# Basic knots

Learn to tie these simple knots to ensure that your rig and hooks are secure.

## Half blood knot

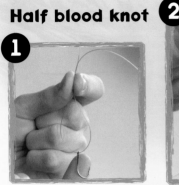

**1** Thread the line through the eye and double up above it.

**2** Twist the hook around eight times. Keep the twists tight and grab the loose end.

**3** Push the hook through the lowest loop between the top of the eye and the first twist.

**4** Push the loose end through the loop you have made. This is called the tuck.

**5** Dampen the knot with a little spit and start to tighten it. Pull the knot down to the eye.

**6** Hold the knot tight for three seconds, then trim it off.

## Figure-eight knot

**1** Make a simple loop at the end of the line.

**2** Hook the loop over itself.

**3** Put your index finger into the large loop and twist it around twice. Then make another half twist.

**4** Tuck the small loop into the larger loop.

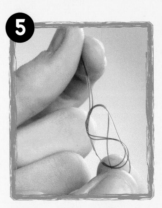

**5** Tighten the knot and a figure eight will form.

**6** Add a little spit before you tighten up.

# Basic techniques

When you are familiar with your rod, tackle, and types of bait, you should practice these techniques at home before you add a hook and head for the water.

## Casting

Casting away from the bank will increase your chance of catching a fish. Always check that no one is standing behind you before you cast.

1. Wind the float to a point of about 2–2.75 in. (5–7 cm) beneath the rod tip and position your rod slightly in front of you to the right.

2. Open the bale arm so that the line is over your index finger.

3. Position the rod at 11 o'clock.

4. Decide where you want to cast, then push the rod tip forward firmly to 1 o'clock, at the same time as releasing the line off your finger. The weight of the tackle will carry the line forward toward the water.

5. When the bait hits the water, wind the float into position, sinking the line.

## Hooking, playing, and landing a fish

When you get a bite, you need to hook the fish. Bites can be quick or slow, gentle, or powerful, so always be prepared for action. If you hook a really big fish, be extremely patient. Carefully use the rod and the reel drag to tire the fish until finally, it is yours. Remember the golden rule: be patient!

**1**

*Be patient as you wait for a bite.*

**2**

*When the float dips below the water, you have a bite.*

**3**

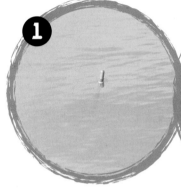

*Lift the rod upward smoothly and firmly—you should feel the fish pulling at the other end.*

**4**

*If it is a bigger fish, keep your rod high and wind in when the fish tires. Sink your landing net into the water.*

**5**

*Wind in until the fish is over the landing net.*

**6**

*Bring the fish into your net.*

### Practice Makes Perfect

Learn by practicing at home. Get a friend to pretend to be the fish, and practice reeling in and giving line as he or she pulls. Learn to get the tension on the reel drag right, to let the line run out without snapping as the "fish" runs away!

# Unhooking and releasing a fish

After landing your fish, great care should be taken to unhook and return it to the water as quickly as possible. Before you put it back in the water, it is a good idea to take a photograph of your catch.

**1**

*Hold the fish in one hand and the top of the hook in the other. Turn the hook around and slide it out.*

## Disgorger Tricks

Ask a fisherman or your tackle dealer to demonstrate how to use a disgorger correctly before you go fishing. It is quick and easy when you know how!

**2**

*If the fish is hooked in the mouth, hold the line tight and slide the disgorger down the line to the hook. Push down on the hook, twist, and remove it.*

**3** Carefully put the fish into the keep net.

**4** Larger fish can be unhooked on a damp fishing mat.

**5** Weigh your catch using a weigh sling. Then, if you like, take a photograph of the fish.

**6** Nurse the fish in the water for a moment before releasing it—do not release it until you feel its strength return.

# Location, location, location

Where you fish will determine what technique you will use. Wherever you fish, make sure you are allowed to do so and obtain the necessary licenses and permits.

## Stillwater fishing

Ponds, lakes, pits, and reservoirs are known as still waters because, unlike rivers, they do not have a current. This makes fishing easier and still water a good place to learn basic fishing skills. Find out all you can about the water you have chosen before you actually go. Take the time to talk to the local tackle shop or visit the water, and talk to fishermen who are on the banks. Check out the cost of tickets, types of fish stocked, the best areas to fish from, and the most popular baits used.

At the waterside, pay attention to the features of the area. It is a good idea to make your own map of the water and keep a record of what you catch and where you catch it. Remember that fish like cover and stillness, so look for features such as reed beds, lily pads, and overhanging trees. Fish close in to the bank using simple float fishing tackle and maggots, attracting the fish with groundbait. For deeper water and distance fishing, ledgering will be a better option. In high summer, where carp are present, surface fishing using bread or dog biscuits is one of the most exciting ways to catch fish.

*This still water is perfect for catching roach, rudd, pike, eels, perch, carp, and tench.*

# Rivers and canals

When you have mastered the basic skills in still waters, you can progress to rivers and canals.

Rivers can be shallow or deep, slow moving or fast, and your tactics will depend on the type of river and the fish you want to catch. Start by fishing close to the bank, so that you can easily control the float with your rod. Stronger currents may require a heavier float to get the bait down to the fish. Remember that the current will move the float downstream and this will require control on your part. Throw in groundbait and loose feed upstream of your swim and in line with the place that you want to fish, so that the offering arrives at the depth and place where you want to fish. In faster water, let the bait roll downstream or wave in the current enticingly.

*This fisherman has thrown some groundbait upstream of where he is fishing. The bait should attract fish, making a catch more likely.*

Canals are usually slow moving and shallow. Fishing either up or downstream of your swim is a good idea to avoid scaring the fish. Canals can look featureless, but you will attract fish into your swim with groundbait and loose feed.

*This canal looks calm and featureless, but there is a wealth of fish lurking below the water's surface.*

# Types of fishing

There are different types of fishing, and depending on the type of fish you are hoping to catch and the location of your swim, you may want to try a variety of methods.

## Surface fishing

Surface fishing is exciting and a great way to catch carp in high summer. Throw in some loose feed and watch for telltale swirls. Cast out and wait—it will be only a matter of time before the carp suck in the bait and fight hard.

## Float fishing

Float fishing uses bright-colored and highly visible floats (see page 9). These allow you to fish your bait at different depths in the water. Floats also help you to detect bites easily. There are many floats to choose from, but you can start with a couple of simple patterns and build up your collection. It is very important to find out the depth of the water in your swim. For this, you can use a special weight called a sinker.

*Use a sinker to find out the depth of water in your swim. The fish may be feeding near the bottom or high up in the water.*

### Floating on the Water

A float is set correctly if you can see just the tip of the float above the water's surface.

22

## Ledgering

Ledgering takes the bait to the bottom of the water. It is used to catch bigger fish and is a great method to use in deep water, for distance fishing, and for fishing a strong current, such as a river.

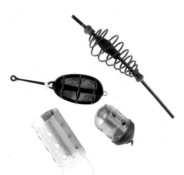

*These are swimfeeders. They are used in ledgering to hold bait at the bottom of the water.*

## Freelining

This stillwater tactic uses no weight except the bait itself. It is successful, especially for carp and tench, because it presents the bait so naturally. Throw in some loose feed, such as corn, near reeds or another fishy spot close to the bank, put a few particles on the hook and lower the bait down. There is no need to cast. Sit back, be patient, and watch the line for sudden movement.

*This is a simple ledger rig. You can vary the hook length to change presentation.*

23

# Fly fishing and sea fishing

Once you have tried coarse fishing and feel confident, then why not try fly fishing for trout, or sea fishing off the coast?

## Fly fishing

There are many places to try fly fishing. Lakes are a good place to learn the basic techniques and are usually stocked with hard-fighting rainbow trout. Some lakes may be stocked with other varieties, too, such as browns, blues, and tigers. Although there are some similarities between coarse and fly fishing, there are also some differences, and you will need to learn a new set of casting in skills.

*Fly fishing is a wonderful branch of the sport. River fishing for trout can get you really close to the fish!*

## Flies

One of the most obvious differences between coarse and fly fishing is that instead of using floats, fly fishermen use flies, which are designed to catch trout. Although some resemble natural flies, other fly patterns do not look anything like real flies! They are very gaudy and work by triggering the trout's attack mode. The trick is to learn about the insect life near the water you are fishing and try to trick the trout by imitating the insects.

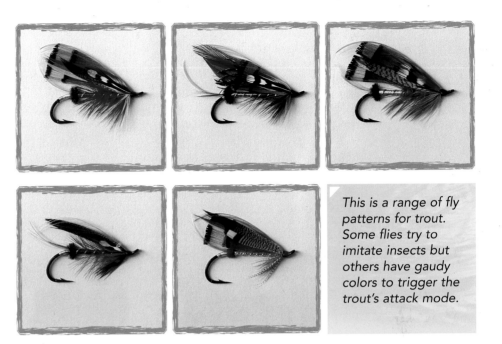

This is a range of fly patterns for trout. Some flies try to imitate insects but others have gaudy colors to trigger the trout's attack mode.

## Sea fishing

If you live near the sea or go there on vacation, then why not try sea fishing? Fish can be caught from jetties, piers, harbor walls, beaches, rocks, and boats. Your equipment will vary depending on the place you want to fish. For example, shorter rods are suitable for harbor walls and jetties, but shore and rock fishing will require something longer. A 15 lb. (7-kg) line loaded onto a fixed-spool reel, along with a small assortment of tackle and bait, will be enough to get you started.

**weights**—these are bigger than freshwater weights so that they can cope with the surges in tides.

**bucket**—you need this to keep your catch.

**beachcaster and deep-sea rod**—sea rods vary in length and power.

**floats**—these are useful for harbor and rock fishing.

**hooks**—hooks for sea fishing are bigger than those used for coarse fishing.

**baits**—fishlike baits are best for sea fishing.

25

# Clubs and competitions

There are fishing clubs all over the world and many cover all aspects of fishing. Some local clubs may support a match-fishing team and others specialize in catching particular fish, such as the Carp Anglers Group, which specializes in carp and has branches all over the United States and Canada. The best way to find a club is to talk to your local tackle shop, visit the library, or do an online search for your local area.

There are many advantages to joining a club. Not only do clubs offer access to "members only" private lakes and stretches of river, but many will also run competitions that you can enter. Much can be learned from more experienced club members, and some clubs offer instruction for more junior or inexperienced members.

*By joining a club, expert help will be on hand. Here, an instructor is offering advice to a girl on where to fish.*

## Competitions

Competition or match fishing is a popular and very successful branch of the sport. There are hundreds of individual and team competitions held every week. Match fishing offers a unique challenge to anglers. At a match, anglers draw a "peg" or swim before the start of the competition and then fish against each other, against other teams, and against the clock to catch the heaviest weight of fish over the day. Match fishing provides every competitor with the chance to be their best at the sport and to learn from those around them. Fishing as part of a team can be a great experience and may lead to strong and lasting friendships—not to mention winning a trophy!

*This carp put up a real fight and was big enough to win a cup for this young angler in a local fishing match.*

# Fish from around the world

Around the world, certain waters are known for their fishing. There is something for everyone, whichever type of fishing you enjoy most.

## Coarse fishing

All over the United States and Canada, carp fishing is really popular, but if you want to fish for really big carp, the best place to do this is Bangkok in Thailand. There, the biggest carp ever caught on a rod and line weighed over 242 pounds (110 kg). Spain's River Ebro is a good place to fish giant catfish. Catfish are predators, and are generally caught using fish baits at night. In 2005, a catfish the size of a grizzly bear was caught in Thailand. The fish was 8.9 feet (2.7 meters) long and weighed 646 lbs. (293 kg). It took a team of anglers over an hour to land the fish.

Although fishermen dream of catching a world record breaker, beating your own record is exciting. This angler was very happy with his own record-breaking carp that weighed just under 22 lbs. (10 kg).

Although this feisty 11-pound (5-kilogram) pike put up a good fight, it was worth it!

## Fly fishing

If you like fly fishing, then you could try going for the giant steelhead of North America. The U.S. record fish was caught in Alaska and weighed in at just over 42 lbs. (19 kg). Giant tarpon are found off the coast of Florida. These enormous fish weigh up to 220 lbs. (100 kg) and are caught from boats in shallow waters called "flats" using fly fishing tackle. Salmon from the Kola Peninsula in Northern Russia are among the best in the world, with fish taken to over 40 lbs. (18 kg) that will test even the strongest tackle.

*This fisherman is nursing the trout he has caught before putting it back.*

## Deep sea fishing

Some of the biggest fish in the world can be caught near the Great Barrier Reef in Australia. There, giant black marlins are common. The biggest caught to date off the reef weighed an incredible 1,212 lbs. (550 kg).

*This big black marlin was caught off the Queensland coast in Australia.*

# Glossary

**Bait**   The things that fish like to eat, such as maggots, corn, or cheese. By using different bait, you will attract different types of fish.

**Bale arm**   An arm that clicks over on the spool of your reel and collects the line onto the spool when you turn the handle.

**Bite**   When a fish takes your bait.

**Boilies**   A specialist, high-protein bait for carp fishing. Boilies are usually colored and strong-flavored.

**Breaking strain**   The limit of strain that a fishing line can take before it snaps. Fishing line comes in a wide variety of strengths, and you can ask your tackle shop for advice on the best line to use for the fish you want to catch.

**Carbon fiber**   A special material that is very light but incredibly strong. Modern fishing rods are made from carbon fiber.

**Coarse fishing**   Fishing for freshwater fish, such as carp.

**Downstream**   The direction in which water naturally flows.

**Drag**   This is the setting on the reel that increases or decreases the level of resistance that the fish feels when taking line. If a strong fish pulls or runs suddenly, drag allows the line to be released without snapping.

**Featureless**   Without any features. Canal waters often look featureless because they are calm and flat.

**Flies**   The lures that fly fishermen use to catch trout and salmon. The flies are made to look like natural flies or they are very bright to provoke the trout's attack mode.

**Floats**   The devices used to present the bait at different levels. They are also used to indicate a bite. Floats are colored on one half, so that you can see them clearly, but they are dull on the other side, so that they do not discourage fish.

**Float fishing**   A fishing tactic that uses floats to show whether or not there is a bite.

**Fly fishing**   Fishing for salmon and trout. Fly fishermen use artificial flies instead of bait.

**Freelining**   A fishing tactic that uses no weight except the bait itself.

**Fresh water**   Rivers, canals, ponds, and lakes are all bodies of fresh water.

**Industrial Revolution**   The time in history in the late eighteenth and early nineteenth centuries when major changes in manufacturing, farming, and transportation took place. After the Revolution, many things were made in factories.

**Keep net**   The net used to keep a fish that you have caught.

**Landing a fish**   When you have caught a fish and have got it safely on the bank, you have landed it.

**Landing net**   The net used to bring the fish to land.

**Ledgering**   A fishing tactic where anglers fish on the bottom of the water.

**Lightning conductor**   Something that allows lightning to travel through it, for example, a fishing rod.

**Match fishing**   Competition fishing where fishermen draw pegs to find out where they need to fish. Prizes are awarded for the biggest fish.

**Playing out**   Once the fish has bitten, it will fight so that it is not caught. Loosening and tightening the line to bring it in is called playing it out.

**Rig**   The line, float, and hook used in fishing.

**Spinning**   A tactic used to catch pike that uses artificial lures, called spinners or plugs, which act like wounded or injured fish in the water, provoking a bite.

**Spool**   This is where the line sits on your reel. Most reels come with more that one spool and they can easily be changed. It is useful to have more than one spool for your reel, with different weights of line for different fish and different conditions.

**Surface fishing**   A fishing tactic where anglers use bait that floats, such as bread crusts or dog biscuits, to catch surface-feeding fish. It is an especially good tactic for catching carp.

**Swimfeeder**   A special device that is used to hold groundbait when you fish on the bottom to get feed close to your hook bait.

**Swims**   Parts along a river or other body of water where you can fish.

**Trace line**   Made of wire or coated plastic, a trace should be used for pike fishing since the fish will not be able to bite through it.

**Upstream**   The opposite direction to the natural flow of water.

**Weir**   A dam built across a river to raise the level of water upstream or regulate its flow.

# Further information and Web Sites

## Books to read

*Hook, Line, and Sinker:
A Beginner's Guide to
Fishing, Boating, and
Watching Water Wildlife*
by Jim Arnosky
(Scholastic Nonfiction, 2005)

*Hook, Line and Sinker:
Everything Kids Want
to Know About Fishing!*
by Italo Labignan
(Key Porter Books, 2007)

*Kids Gone Fishin': The
Freshwater Angler*
by Dave Maas
(Creative Publishing
International, 2001)

## Web Sites

Due to the changing nature of
Internet links, PowerKids Press has
developed an online list of Web sites
related to the subject of this book.
This site is updated regularly. Please
use this link to access this list:
www.powerkidslinks.com/outd/fish

# index